Puppy's First Year

Miriam Fields-Babineau

A trio of West Highland White Terrier puppies.

© T.F.H. Publications, Inc.

Distributed in the UNITED STATES to the Pet Trade by T.F.H. Publications, Inc., 1 TFH Plaza, Neptune City, NJ 07753; on the Internet at www.tfh.com; in CANADA by Rolf C. Hagen Inc., 3225 Sartelon St., Montreal, Quebec H4R 1E8; Pet Trade by H & L Pet Supplies Inc., 27 Kingston Crescent, Kitchener, Ontario N2B 2T6; in ENGLAND by T.F.H. Publications, PO Box 74, Havant PO9 5TT; in AUSTRALIA AND THE SOUTH PACIFIC by T.F.H. (Australia), Pty. Ltd., Box 149, Brookvale 2100 N.S.W., Australia; in NEW ZEALAND by Brooklands Aquarium Ltd., 5 McGiven Drive, New Plymouth, RD1 New Zealand; in SOUTH AFRICA by Rolf C. Hagen S.A. (PTY.) LTD., P.O. Box 201199, Durban North 4016, South Africa; in JAPAN by T.F.H. Publications. Published by T.F.H. Publications, Inc.

MANUFACTURED IN THE
UNITED STATES OF AMERICA
BY T.F.H. PUBLICATIONS, INC.

In a quiet moment this Sheltie puppy stops to smell the petunias.

Contents

Photo Credits: Miriam Fields-Babineau, Wil de Veer, Isabelle Francais, Chet Jezierski, Pets by Paulette, Judith E. Strom, Karen J. Taylor, and Linda Willard.

Puppies are irresistible and will make wonderful additions to your family!

SELECTING THE RIGHT PUPPY FOR YOUR FAMILY

You've decided to get a puppy. Fantastic! Where do you begin? Have you researched the breeds? Found a breeder? Are you and your family ready for this big responsibility? Is your house ready? What about a name? For ease of identification and association, we'll refer to the puppy in this book as Snoopy.

So many questions. Where does one begin looking for the answers? Right here!

Let's begin with finding the right puppy for your family and lifestyle. Where do we go? Directly to the source—the breeder.

Learning about Snoopy's parents is the first step to understanding your puppy. Once you know which breed you want, you can locate reputable breeders by contacting the American Kennel Club in New York City, New York. They have a huge list of breeders. And, if the breeder you contact does not have puppies, they often know of other breeders who do. Breed-ers network among themselves. This way they can coordinate specific breedings and schedules to ensure good products—well-bred puppies.

The best place to learn about your puppy's future temperament is to interact with its parents. Think of the parents as the dog your puppy will become. Most often you can meet the dam (mother), if not the sire (father). Watch closely as the dam interacts with unfamiliar people and children. Does she

Your puppy will have a good start in life if his parents are happy and well adjusted. Try to see the dam and the sire of the puppy you are considering.

5

The apple doesn't fall very far from the tree! Often the temperament of a puppy will be much like her parents. A Mastiff mom and her pups.

allow strangers to touch her puppies? If so, she will most likely pass on the good temperament to her offspring. If not, you may want to inquire about her behavior. Has she had a bad experience in the past or is she always possessive or overly shy? Some mothers will be insecure about strangers interacting with her puppies. If so, the breeder will make certain she is not with them when you visit. Take the time to visit with her. Keep in mind that the puppies possess half their mother's genes. If the dam has questionable behavior you may not want to purchase the pup.

If the sire is on the premises, take time to visit with him also. Check for the same types of behavior aberrations. Does the father allow you and

your family to pet him? Is he safe with children? Can you hug and kiss him without his getting nervous or otherwise upset? Provided he passes all these tests, you can be assured that the puppy will receive his good nature.

If the sire is not on the premises, be certain to find out his location and contact his owner. Ask the owner questions about the sire's health, behavior, and vocation. A good sire or dam will also be a dog that has earned titles in one or more dog sports. You can learn this by looking at the dog's pedigree. Beside his name you will see either Ch., meaning he is a conformation champion; CD, CDX, or UD, obedience titles; TD, TDX, tracking titles; FLDCH, FCH, WC, WD, field or hunting titles; SchH,

schutzhund; or CGC, canine good citizen. To be absolutely certain of the sire though, you should go visit with him. You can also learn about him through contact with the AKC. They have records of his pedigree and titles. Testing the parent's behavior is of foremost importance because you do not want to bring home a puppy that is genetically aggressive.

Another tact is to contact the owners of previous litters. They can tell you even more about the breeding. If you receive positive input from them, you can be certain your puppy will be of good genetic stock. Personality is one thing, but a healthy puppy is equally important.

The next thing you should do is check the parent's health

records. If purebred, both parents should have OFA, CERF, and VWD certification, which clears the dog of dysplasia, heart and eye problems, and other congenital defects. Regardless of the breed's purity, a veterinarian's health certificate should also indicate gum problems as well as internal dysfunctions. Watch the parents as they move. Do they limp or walk funny? Be especially critical of their hind legs and hips. A healthy dog has free movement, without excessive swing of the hind end.

fected and the water should be low enough for them to reach but not surrounded by mud. Their bedding should be changed three times per day, so you shouldn't see a lot of mess. Puppies kept inside a home, which is common with smaller breeds, may have

A litter of puppies may be adorable, but be certain to educate yourself about the responsibilities of owning a dog before you bring one home. A litter of Golden Retrievers.

be presented and should state the parents are free of worms, fleas, and respiratory illness. There are also a few things you can check for by just looking at the parents. Is the coat clean and shiny? If you see white flakes and feel a dry coat, this might be a sign of malnutrition. Is the dog too skinny or too fat? You should see a waistline on any healthy dog. Does the dog have bad breath? Bad breath can

One of the most obvious means of ensuring you receive a healthy puppy is to inspect the kennel. If the pups are in a pen, is it clean? If the puppies are inside the breeder's home, are they contained in a clean area or allowed to run loose? A good environment for puppies is a large enclosure where they have access to shelter and outdoors. The surface should be easily cleaned and disin-

more socialization, especially if the breeder has children. No child can keep their hands off of cute puppies.

An especially diligent breeder will begin teaching the puppies where to do their "business." An area filled with wood shavings or sand is provided for the pups and the breeder watches to be sure they go there when relieving themselves. This will make housetraining easier on you, for the puppies will have already been conditioned to not mess on the carpet or floor.

All puppies should begin their socialization training before they even open their eyes. The breeder should take time to pick up each dog, touch it all over, and give kisses and raspberries on the belly (optional). Background music and occasional noises will ensure your pup is not afraid of loud sounds.

Good breeders will always send you home with a large packet of information containing the parent's pedigrees, health certifications, championship certificates, and a record of your puppy's worming and inoculations. They will also discuss how to feed your pup and which brand of food they were using. This is very important, because if you switch Snoopy's food too abruptly he may have intestinal problems. If you need to switch his food, do it very slowly, over the course of a week, gradually increasing the new food into the mixture each day.

Before taking your puppy home, be sure to check him for signs of good health. He will have clean eyes and ears, a round belly, and a glossy, soft coat. When active, he will be able to trot around, fall, roll, swing his head, and bite your shoelace. Most puppies will jump on you and mouth your fingers. Some, but not all, will bark and growl when playing. Sit back and watch

Rub-a-dub-dub, three Schipperkes in a tub! Healthy puppies should have bright eyes and shiny coats, like this bucket full of Schipperkes.

your pup playing with the others. There's much you can learn about both his health and personality through simple observation.

Observing your puppy interacting with his siblings is the first step of temperament testing. Every puppy should be tested to ensure he goes to the right home. Not only are there distinct differences between breeds, but also within the breeds. Every puppy is an individual.

BREED CHARACTERISTICS

Before we discuss the individual breed characteristics, you should be aware of gender differences. There is a distinct difference between male and female dogs. These are not always consistent from breed to breed and individuals can often show exceptions from the norm. However, when choosing a dog you should be aware of the following.

Female dogs tend to be easier to housetrain, obedience train, and have fewer behavioral problems. They also tend to want more affection. Male dogs may be more excitable, destructive, and harder to housetrain. They also tend to be more playful, better watchdogs, and are more likely to be dominant over their owner. Male dogs also may tend to be more aggressive toward other dogs, more territorial, and have a higher incidence of snapping at children. The male dog's behavior patterns make it a necessity to neuter them as soon as they reach sexual maturity. This reduces the negative behaviors, making them better pets.

Another thing to take into consideration when choosing the gender of your pup is how particular you are about your yard. A female dog will urinate in puddles, thus causing dead grass patches, while a male dog will usually lift his leg, which may destroy shrubs. Keep in mind that any dog likes to dig and race around, so don't expect to have a nice landscape in the same area where your dog plays.

A few generalities can be assumed when looking for the perfect dog. Size, maintenance, and ease of care are a few of them. When looking at energy level, ease of training, and social ability, you will need to look at specific breeds.

Toy dogs can live in tight quarters and do not need much outdoor exercise. They work well in apartments and are easy to maintain when at home or while traveling.

Small dogs can do well in tight quarters but do need to have a little run at least once per day. They do require some training and are easy to clean up after both at home and while traveling.

Medium dogs require more exercise than a single walk. They need to play outside several times per day and must have obedience training. They are a little harder to clean up after but still do well in semi-small quarters such as town homes and condominiums.

Large dogs must have a yard to play in, regular walks, and obedience training. You will need to stimulate them with activities and allow them to play with other dogs on a regular basis. They are more work to clean up after, and

offer a higher nuisance level than a small dog.

Huge dogs must have a yard and be walked daily. As with all dogs, they require obedience training. They can be very difficult to clean up after both inside and out and are difficult to travel with (they take up the entire back seat). Many large breeds such as Saint Bernards and Newfoundlands tend to drool a lot. This can be very annoying to the immaculate housekeeper.

Also keep in mind that the larger the dog, the more expensive he will be to maintain. He will consume more food, may cost more to groom, neuter, and if you must leave him home when you travel, more to board.

The coat length of the breed will decide how difficult the dog will be to maintain. Obviously, the longer the coat, the more time consuming and possibly costly the grooming.

A smooth-coated dog will require little maintenance

other than a weekly grooming and examination to ensure against pests, lumps, and changes in physical health. Examples of smooth-coated dogs are Doberman Pinschers, Beagles, and Labrador Retrievers.

A dog with a short coat will need to be brushed several times per week. Examples of short-coated dogs are Corgis, Chihuahuas, and Chesapeake Bay Retrievers. As with the smooth-coated dog, he should be checked weekly for dermal changes.

A dog with a medium coat such as a German Shepherd, Siberian Husky, or Borzoi will need to be groomed every other day. Dogs with a medium coat that feathers at the legs such as Spaniels, Golden Retrievers, and Setters will require regular grooming at least every other day and, if a Spaniel, clipping every six weeks.

Dogs with a wiry coat often require regular trips to the groomer for clipping, as well

Whether male or female, any well-socialized puppy will make an equally loving, devoted, and trainable companion. Three Akita siblings smile for the camera.

It is important to remember that your puppy's needs will vary according to what breed you take home. A long-haired breed that grows to be very large, like these Great Pyrenees, will require extensive grooming and plenty of room to roam when he grows up.

as regular grooming at least every other day. Examples of wiry-coated dogs include Cairn Terriers, Airedale Terriers, and Schnauzers.

Curly-coated dogs such as Poodles, Kerry Blue Terriers, Wheaton Terriers, and Water Spaniels require trips to the groomer every six weeks.

A long-coated dog will take up much time both at home and at the groomer. This includes breeds such as Afghans, Old English Sheepdogs, and full-coated Shih Tzu and Maltese. Burrs, leaves, and other outdoor debris will be caught in their coats so you should check them each time you bring them indoors, especially after a hike in the mountains or woods.

On the following pages is a list of breeds according to energy level, trainability, and sociability. Energy level

pertains to how much play drive and excitability the breed exhibits. Trainability means the dog responds well to positive training techniques. Sociability means the dog easily accepts other people and dogs. This can further be differentiated by separating their social behavior with dogs and that with people, for many breeds will or will not easily accept one over the other.

Remember, there are individuals which may not fall into these categorized lists, but when looking for a permanent addition to your family you want to make the wisest choice possible and a general guideline is helpful.

A PERFECT FIT

Before you choose a puppy you need to take into consideration your home, family,

and lifestyle. If you work all day, for example, you don't want to get a puppy that is destructive and in dire need of attention. Below is a sample listing of lifestyles and the types of dogs that might do well in that environment.

A single, working person: You want a dog that trains easily, doesn't mind being left alone, is a good watch dog, but not an excessive barker. If you are an assertive person you can handle a dominant personality in your dog.

A couple that both work: The criteria is similar to a single working person, however, you can handle a dog with a little more demand for affection and excitability because there are two of you to offer him attention. Provided one of you is assertive, you can handle a dominant personality.

A single person or a couple with one person that stays at home: The type of dog depends most on the personality of the person who remains home. If the person is consistent and assertive, any dog will do. If not, be sure to choose an amenable dog. If the person is active, then choose an active, energetic dog. A dog that has much demand for affection would work well in this environment.

Elderly or retired couple or single person: This dog should be of low energy, very amenable, nondominant, easily trained, and demand attention. Size should also be an issue because a large, strong dog can be dangerous. A very submissive dog would do well in this type of quiet atmosphere.

A family with young children: A dominant dog would be very wrong in this situation. The dog should be easily trained, with high energy levels and a high demand for affection, but not the type that jumps up and snaps. A dog that easily submits to the owner would work well.

A puppy can be likened to having another child. You can make sure Snoopy will fit in by doing the following tempera-

Personalities will vary among puppies, so be sure to choose one that will fit with your lifestyle. This little girl and her Akita seem perfectly matched!

ment tests before bringing him home from the breeder or pet shop.

Temperament Test #1
Watch your puppy playing. If he:
1. Jumps on and bites other pups—dominant.
2. Rolls onto his back when

jumped on—submissive.
3. Does not give in to pups jumping on him. Instead, he growls and jumps on his aggressor—very dominant.
4. Does not often join in the fun. Watches close by—independent.
5. Hides in a corner—fearful.

Temperament Test #2
Play with your pup in an area away from the other pups. While playing with him touch his ears, feet, tail, tummy, and mouth.
1. Puppy bites you when you touch a specific area—dominant-aggressive.
2. Puppy jumps on you and grabs your fingers—dominant-playful.
3. Puppy squirms away and goes to explore—independent.
4. Puppy allows you to touch him anywhere—amiable-submissive.
5. Puppy squeals and squirms away—fearful.

Temperament Test #3
Drop your keys or a big book nearby.
1. Puppy barks and goes after object—dominant.
2. Puppy barks but remains in one place looking at source of noise—watchful but not aggressive.
3. Puppy looks at noise then returns to playing—alert but not fearful.

ENERGY LEVEL

BREED	LOW	MODERATE	HIGH
Afghan Hound		X	
Airedale Terrier			X
Akita	X		
Alaskan Malamute	X		
Australian Shepherd			X
Basset Hound	X		
Beagle		X	
Bichon Frise	X		
Bloodhound	X		
Boston Terrier		X	
Boxer			X
Brittany Spaniel			X
Bulldog	X		
Cairn Terrier			X
Chesapeake Bay Retriever			X
Chihauhua		X	
Chow Chow	X		
Cocker Spaniel		X	
Collie		X	
Dachshund		X	
Dalmatian			X
Doberman Pinscher		X	
English Springer Spaniel			X
German Shepherd Dog			X
Golden Retriever			X
Great Dane	X		
Irish Setter			X
Keeshond		X	
Labrador Retiever			X
Lhasa Apso		X	
Maltese		X	
Newfoundland	X		
Norwegian Elkhound		X	
Old English Sheepdog		X	
Pekingese		X	
Pomeranian			X
Miniature Poodle		X	
Standard Poodle			X
Toy Poodle			X
Pug	X		
Rottweiler		X	
Saint Bernard	X		
Samoyed		X	
Miniature Schnauzer			X
Standard Schnauzer			X
Scottish Terrier			X
Shetland Sheepdog		X	
Shih Tzu		X	
Siberian Husky			X
Weimaraner		X	
Pembroke Welsh Corgi		X	
West Highland Wt. Terrier			X
Yorkshire Terrier			X

TRAINABILITY

BREED	LOW	MODERATE	HIGH
Afghan Hound	X		
Airedale Terrier		X	
Akita	X		
Alaskan Malamute		X	
Australian Shepherd			X
Basset Hound	X		
Beagle	X		
Bichon Frise		X	
Bloodhound	X		
Boston Terrier		X	
Boxer			X
Brittany Spaniel			X
Bulldog		X	
Cairn Terrier		X	
Chesapeake Bay Retriever		X	
Chihauhua			X
Chow Chow	X		
Cocker Spaniel		X	
Collie			X
Dachshund	X		
Dalmatian	X		
Doberman Pinscher			X
English Springer Spaniel		X	
German Shepherd Dog			X
Golden Retriever			X
Great Dane		X	
Irish Setter		X	
Keeshond		X	
Labrador Retiever			X
Lhasa Apso		X	
Maltese		X	
Newfoundland		X	
Norwegian Elkhound		X	
Old English Sheepdog	X		
Pekingese		X	
Pomeranian		X	
Miniature Poodle			X
Standard Poodle		X	
Toy Poodle		X	
Pug		X	
Rottweiler		X	

Breed			
Saint Bernard		X	
Samoyed	X		
Miniature Schnauzer		X	
Standard Schnauzer	X		
Scottish Terrier			X
Shetland Sheepdog			X
Shih Tzu		X	
Siberian Husky	X		
Weimaraner		X	
Pembroke Welsh Corgi			X
West Highland Wt. Terrier		X	
Yorkshire Terrier		X	

SOCIABILITY

BREED	LOW	MODERATE	HIGH
Afghan Hound	X		
Airedale Terrier		X	
Akita	X		
Alaskan Malamute		X	
Australian Shepherd		X	
Basset Hound		X	
Beagle			X
Bichon Frise		X	
Bloodhound		X	
Boston Terrier		X	
Boxer			X
Brittany Spaniel		X	
Bulldog			X
Cairn Terrier		X	
Chesapeake Bay Retriever	X		
Chihauhua	X		
Chow Chow	X		
Cocker Spaniel		X	
Collie			X
Dachshund	X		
Dalmatian	X		
Doberman Pinscher		X	
English Springer Spaniel		X	
German Shepherd Dog		X	
Golden Retriever			X
Great Dane			X
Keeshond			X
Irish Setter			X
Labrador Retiever			X
Lhasa Apso	X		
Maltese	X		
Newfoundland		X	
Norwegian Elkhound		X	
Old English Sheepdog			X
Pekingese	X		

Breed				
Pomeranian			X	
Miniature Poodle				X
Standard Poodle				X
Toy Poodle			X	
Pug			X	
Rottweiler	X			
Saint Bernard			X	
Samoyed	X			
Miniature Schnauzer	X			
Standard Schnauzer	X			
Scottish Terrier			X	
Shetland Sheepdog			X	
Shih Tzu				X
Siberian Husky	X			
Weimaraner			X	
Pembroke Welsh Corgi				X
West Highland Wt. Terrier			X	
Yorkshire Terrier	X			

The temperament of the puppy you choose is an important consideration. This little Golden Retriever appears relaxed and laid back!

13

Most puppies require some vegetable matter in their diet. The Carrot Bone™ is a wonderful way to provide your puppy with the nutrition he needs in a fun-to-chew, healthy way!

4. Puppy is frightened and runs a short distance away, but returns to play within a minute—fearful, but not overly so.

5. Puppy runs and hides—fearful.

Temperament Test #4

Put a toy near the puppy.

1. Puppy attacks toy and takes it away from you—possessive, possibly dominant.

2. Puppy goes to toy and plays with it where it lies—independent.

3. Puppy plays with toy and carries it around—playful.

4. Puppy brings toy to you to play with him—dependent and playful.

5. Puppy runs and hides—fearful.

Temperament Test #5

Throw the toy.

1. Puppy goes after toy and takes it farther away—possessive.

2. Puppy goes after toy and plays with it there—independent.

3. Puppy goes after toy and brings it back dropping it near you—playful and dependent.

4. Puppy brings toy back to play tug-of-war—playful.

5. Puppy ignores toy or approaches cautiously—fearful.

Temperament Test #6

Roll the puppy onto his back and hold him there for ten seconds.

1. Puppy squirms and bites at you until you let him up—dominant.

2. Puppy squirms a while and then relaxes—playful, amenable.

3. Puppy instantly relaxes—submissive.

4. Puppy yelps and squirms, possibly bites at you, but eventually settles—fearful.

Temperament Test #7

Walk backwards clapping your hands, speaking in a high, enticing tone of voice. Once you are 20 feet away, crouch down.

1. Puppy comes to you, ears forward, and attacks your feet—dominant.

2. Puppy comes then goes in opposite direction—independent.

3. Puppy comes to you and jumps up—playful.

4. Puppy comes to you and watches you—cooperative and easily trained.

5. Puppy watches from a far corner, or puppy comes crawling on his belly, lies down when he arrives, and possibly whimpers—fearful.

If the puppy shows dominance in any of these tests he may do well in a family with one or two assertive people, but not with children or the elderly. This dog must have consistent training, with daily work with his owners. If he is allowed one infraction, he will try for more. Approach his training with firmness but never lose your temper or become aggressive.

The independent puppy will also not do well in a family with children, although he may do well with a sedate elderly person or family without children. He would never satisfy the activity levels associated with rambunctious youngsters. With consistent, patient training he might become more dependent on his owners, making him a good pet.

The fearful dog should not be in a family with children. He might do well with a single working person or couple that have a quiet home life. Approach his training in a positive manner with lots of rewards.

The playful, amiable, and submissive dog will be great with children, active families, and singles, but not with the elderly or with someone who works long hours leaving him home alone. He needs to have attention and love and must be watched or may get into mischief. This type of puppy will need positive, persistent training.

Now that you know what type of puppy you want, you need to prepare your home and schedule for the new arrival.

THE PUPPY COMES HOME

Bringing home a puppy is similar to bringing home a newborn baby. There's so much to do! Where to begin? We need to know what we need, how to baby-proof, er...puppy-proof your home, and the entire family must be aware of their roles and the rules of the household.

Let's start with a list of things we need before our new family member comes home. We have to consider bedding, crates, training supplies, grooming supplies, and toys.

Puppies chew. They teeth from the time you get them until they reach nine months of age. The last thing you want to do is spend lots of money on a beautifully carved wooden dog bed with a feather mattress. Puppies prefer anything with the scent of their pack members (your family) on it. A towel, old coat, or blanket will work just fine. If you must buy a bed, get something that your pup is less likely to chew, such as a PVC pipe bed. These are easy to clean and not as tasty as a foam bed with a designer cover. They are also very comfortable and lightweight.

Every pup needs a crate. Crates may look like awful, closed-in places to us, but not to the pup. A crate is a place of security—a den. Puppies are happy to feel the crate sides all around them and will be less likely to mess in the crate, making housetraining much easier. Make sure the crate is not much bigger than your puppy. If your pup is going to be large, you don't

Puppies are particularly social creatures and need the company of other puppies when young. Like these Rottweilers, the more people and animals he meets, the better socialized your dog will become.

want to keep buying new crates, so you should purchase a crate divider. This allows you to make the crate larger as your pup grows.

Every puppy needs a collar and leash. While these things are not really used until your pup undergoes training, he needs to get used to their feel. The collar should be made of soft material. The most economical collar is one that adjusts

as your puppy grows. If your puppy currently has a 14-inch neck but will grow to have a 24-inch neck, you will go through several adjustable collars. However, two adjustable collars are better than five non-adjustable collars. When your pup is fully grown you can invest in that beautiful leather collar with the silver and brass dog bone designs.

The collar should not be on your puppy when he is left alone. This can be dangerous, for he can get a paw stuck inside or get the buckle caught on something. The collar should also be removed if your puppy is playing with another pup. Puppies mouth each other on the neck and it is easy for a little one's lower jaw to be caught on a collar.

The leash should be at least four feet long, preferably six feet, made of cotton or nylon. Allow your little one to drag the leash around the house or yard, but do not allow children to pull on it. Keep in mind, Snoopy knows nothing about walking on a leash and forcing him to walk by dragging him around will have very negative results.

Grooming your puppy on a specially made grooming table with a harness will help to keep him safe and still during your sessions. This Old English Sheepdog shows how it's done.

All puppies need to acclimate to being brushed and having their nails clipped and ears and teeth cleaned. You will need a soft bristle body brush, nail clipper, ear wipes, tooth brush and special toothpaste. If your dog has long hair, a comb should be added to your grooming kit.

The types of toys you choose should be both safe and enticing to your pup. Puppies will prefer anything they can sink their teeth into. To avoid having their teeth sink into your favorite pair of running shoes, provide the pup with a variety of toys which stimulate his gums and mind. A good variety includes Nylabones®, Gumabones®, Plaque Attackers™, and if a small breed, you can add plush toys and squeaky toys. Watch carefully as your pup plays with these latter toys. If he begins to chew up the squeaky toys or plush toys, promptly remove them. As your puppy grows he'll prob-

ably like chasing balls and Frisbees™. Tennis and racket balls are favorites and there are several types of Frisbees™, such as the Nylabone® Frisbee™, on the market.

The toys should be rotated daily. This provides more stimulation for your pup. As with a human child, puppies tend to play more with the toys if you play with them. There may be special toys that you bring out only when you are going to play with him, such as a canvas toy, pull toy or, if you plan on showing in obedience or field trials, a dumbbell or canvas dummy.

Once you have everything in place, sit down and talk to the entire family about their responsibilities and how to involve the puppy in your life. For the puppy to learn quickly and be happy the entire family will need to be consistent, patient, and stick to schedules and rules. It would not be fair to the pup for someone to allow him on the furniture when the house rules forbid it. Lay down the laws and make sure everybody will abide by them.

A good set of rules are the following:

1. Snoopy should never be allowed on the furniture, unless you intend to always allow him up there, regardless of how muddy his paws might be.

2. Whenever someone wishes to play with the puppy, they go down to his level on the floor. Never play with the puppy if he jumps up for attention. This teaches him to jump on you.

3. If the puppy is out of his crate he must be watched at all times. This means a constant eye, not an eye that

wanders back and forth to the television. All it takes is two seconds for the puppy to go potty on the carpet.

4. Whoever has puppy-watch duty must take him to his relief area every hour. He must also be taken there after napping, playing, and eating. Draw up a schedule depicting when he eats and when you observe he must go potty. This will help others know when it's "time."

5. No one should play with the puppy's mouth. This teaches him to bite.

6. Your puppy should always wear a leash when outside.

7. Never feed your puppy table scraps or anything that his sensitive tummy is unfamiliar with.

8. Keep your puppy confined in his crate when no one can watch him.

9. Everyone must be consistent. This is of the utmost importance and makes the difference between owning a well-behaved family member and eventually wanting to find him another home.

Be sure to provide your puppy with plenty of safe toys to play with. The Nylabone® Gumabone™ is just the thing for these German Shepherds!

It is important to remember that when your puppy is young he will need you to reassure and help him through his first few days at your home. These two Chocolate Lab puppies look like they've found their perfect guide!

10. Make sure everyone in the family *wants* the puppy. It can be very stressful if one person does not want the puppy and the puppy becomes destructive. It has been known to ruin relationships and send puppies to animal shelters. Everyone *must* want this new baby and everyone *must* be involved in his life—good times and bad.

Puppies are not toys. They are living things that can be time consuming and expensive. Once you make the decision to get a puppy, you must commit to ownership for the life of the dog.

There are ways to prevent your puppy from being de-structive and from frustrating you. Simply puppy-proof your home.

First, a young puppy should only be allowed to be loose in a limited area. Allowing him freedom throughout your home is both overwhelming to him and asking for problems. Place his crate in an area of your home where you spend most of your time, such as the kitchen or den. Gate off the other areas of the house. Close doors to bedrooms and bathrooms. Remove anything breakable from the floor and low tables. Never leave food on a coffee or end table. If you don't need something that is plugged in, remove the plug and put it out of reach. If electrical cords *must* remain in place, spray them with a bitter-tasting repellent or coat them with tabasco sauce. Place all plants out of reach. Make sure all shoes (those not on your feet) are removed from the area. All children's toys should also be removed. Scatter puppy toys around the area. While your puppy is loose, play with him and keep him occupied.

Sticking to these rules and schedules will put you and Snoopy well on your way to a great relationship.

A young puppy will not know the difference between good and bad behavior. It is up to you, the owner, to teach him what is acceptable in your household.

PUPPY CARE

FEEDING

While Snoopy is with his mother he nurses as often as every three hours. This is important for the transfer of nutrients for normal development. Puppies require far more protein and fat than an adult dog because they have a quick metabolism. Also, a puppy's stomach capacity is not large enough to hold sufficient food to contain all his daily requirements. Thus you will need to feed Snoopy four times per day for the first week or two. When Snoopy is three months of age you can decrease the feedings to three times per day, and when he reaches five months you can reduce further to his normal two feedings per day, which you should continue the remainder of his life. Fresh water should be available at all times.

Puppies under three months of age still have little teeth and therefore need to have their food moistened with warm water or milk. Do not overdo the milk, however, or Snoopy might have digestive problems because milk acts as a laxative. Allow him a half hour to eat. Discard all uneaten portions.

Feed Snoopy on a regular schedule. Also try to teach him where to eat, such as at his bowl on the kitchen floor or in his crate. If your puppy tends to be easily distracted and does not eat well, you should feed him in a quiet place, such as his crate. This would also be helpful if Snoopy prefers to take his kibble to your carpet before consuming it.

If your breeder has not recommended a specific food

A healthy puppy will look forward to mealtime and have a voracious appetite. This Golden Retriever pup reaches in to give herself a hand!

for your pup (most breeders will), then check with your veterinarian. Most any type of puppy food will work, but there are certain breeds that remain healthier on a specific brand. When you read the label make sure the protein level is very high, for puppies need a minimum of 25 percent protein in their diets. A protein level of 35-43 percent would be even better. This is necessary for normal growth and the production of antibodies to aid in the healing of wounds.

If your puppy has a sensitive digestive system you should feed him a chicken or lamb and rice food. Buy a quality food that does not have a lot of fillers and chemical preservatives. Add a bit of oil, such as Linatone, to his food to maintain a soft, shiny coat. Brewer's yeast and garlic is also a plus for helping his digestive system, coat, and, best of all, in repelling fleas. If your puppy food does not have a high-protein level, add cottage cheese or yogurt daily and a soft-boiled egg once a week.

Often the feeding directions on the food containers are accurate. However, every puppy is an individual and while some may do well at the specified amounts, others will either become obese or not carry enough weight. Keep an eye on your pup. While you do want to see a bit of rolly polly, you don't want him to be overweight because this can cause bone and heart problems as he grows. Do a weekly check by running your hands down his spine and sides. This way you get a feel for his proper weight. You should barely be able to feel his bones and there should be a waist line after his rib cage. You should not see protruding hip bones.

In early life, puppies receive most of their nourishment from their mother. Once they arrive at your home, be sure their diet includes all the nutrients they need to keep growing.

One of the fundamentals of good health throughout your dog's life is a sound, healthy diet. Photo courtesy of Nutro Products, Inc.

Snoopy should remain on his puppy food until he reaches six months of age. At this time, switch him over to a maintenance food. This is extremely important if Snoopy is a large breed because they tend to get panosteitis, or growing pains. The symptoms range from moderate limping to severe lameness. It is caused because his body is unable to keep up with the fast growth of his bones. On X-rays it appears as an opaque white color, usually on the long bones of the legs. It can affect any of his legs at any time. In fact, the limping often switches from leg to leg. Growing pains can be noticed as young as four months of age to as old as two years. The only cure is for your pup to grow into his bones and muscles. You can give him an aspirin if he is in a lot of pain. Switching Snoopy from the high-protein diet that promotes growth to something that may slow him down a bit might prevent growing pains.

Even though you may be switching only from a puppy to a maintenance formula, not the brand of food, do so gradually. A quick switch can cause digestive disorders. Mix the food together for up to a week, gradually increasing the ratio of new to old before feeding only the new food.

GROOMING

Regardless of Snoopy's breed, he should be groomed. This not only promotes cleanliness but also enhances the bond between you and your dog. Snoopy needs to learn to be touched from his nose to his toes. Learning this while young will make grooming and veterinary examinations easier.

The types of brushes you need depend on the breed. If Snoopy has a short coat you'll need a short bristle brush or a grooming glove. For a long-haired breed, use a widely spaced comb with blunt teeth and a long bristle brush. You will also need blunt end scissors and canine nail clippers. Ear wipes for ear cleaning are also a necessity, especially for dogs with floppy ears.

Snoopy must get used to bathing on a regular basis— every 10 to 14 days if he is an indoor dog and once a month if he lives outdoors. While a small dog or puppy can be washed in a basin, a larger

Never allow your puppy to remain wet after a bath. Wrap him in a clean towel and dry him thoroughly.

Take special care when cleaning your puppy's delicate ears—wipe them gently with cleanser and a moist cloth.

breed will need to be washed in the bathtub. Dry skin will not be a problem provided you continue putting oil in his food. Stick to shampoos made specifically for puppies. Always groom your pup before bathing and stick some cotton in his ears to prevent the water from entering the ear canals. If you plan on washing his face, place a gentle ophthalmic ointment in his eyes for protection. Make sure Snoopy is completely dry before allowing him outside.

Nail trimming should be done every six weeks. This is very important, because long nails can cause the foot to splay or spread, causing lameness. If Snoopy has his dewclaws (the claws higher up his leg) then these can curl around and pierce his skin, as well as rip clothing if he jumps up.

Before trimming his nails, look closely at them. They will appear like hooks. You must be careful not to clip the quick, which contains a blood vessel. If cut, it can bleed a lot. Be sure to have styptic powder on hand, just in case. If your pup's nails are white, the quick will be easy to spot. It appears pink under the nail. Clip just before the pink. For black nails, clip little pieces at a time until the hook-like part is gone. As you can see it is very important for Snoopy to remain still and relaxed for nail clipping.

Ear cleaning should be done at least once a month. There are some breeds however that require the procedure more often. Spaniels and

If you accustom your puppy to regular grooming procedures, like nail clipping, at an early age, he will come to think of it as an enjoyable experience.

Puppies with long, voluminous coats, like these Bearded Collies, will require extensive grooming to look their best.

but do not enter the ear canal.

Some dogs have lots of hair in their ears. This can disrupt the air flow and cause moisture to be trapped in the ear canal. Take a pair of tweezers and pluck the hairs that easily come out. Do not continue tugging on stubborn hairs. This can hurt!

Eye cleaning is important for dogs with protruding eyes, such as many of the toy breeds. Never allow hair to get in their eyes because this can cause major irritation. Monitor the eyes for redness or discharge. Clean often with eye drops and a damp soft cloth. It would be a good idea to take your dog for grooming every six weeks and request careful clipping around the eyes.

Something most pet owners often ignore is dental care. Your pet's teeth are as important to him as yours are to

retrievers, due to spending much time in water and having floppy ears, should have their ears inspected and cleaned more often. Part of the inspection should include smelling the ears. A rancid odor can mean infection.

Begin the procedure by wrapping an ear wipe or a soft cloth dampened with mineral oil around your index finger. Gently clean the outer ear. A cotton swab also soaked in mineral oil can reach a little deeper,

It's as important for our animal friends to have healthy teeth and gums as it is for us. Fortunately, maintaining oral care is getting easier and easier for pet owners. Now there's a taste-free, easy-to-use gel that will keep pets' teeth clean, reduce tartar build up and eliminate breath odor. Photo courtesy of Breath Friend™ / American Media Group.

You and your puppy can enjoy hours of fun with a Nylafloss™. It's a great tug toy and it does wonders for your puppy's dental health by massaging his gums and literally flossing between his teeth, loosening plaque and tartar buildup.

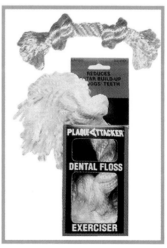

This lovely Keeshond duo obviously enjoys showing off their good grooming for the camera!

There are several toys on the market which will help Snoopy's teeth in tartar reduction. Dry food also helps reduce tartar buildup.

Small breeds have a tendency to need more dental attention than larger breeds. Some will need to have a veterinarian attend to their tooth scaling under anesthesia to ensure that their gums and teeth remain healthy. You will not have to have this done as often if you maintain a regular dental cleaning schedule and proper diet.

HEALTH CARE

Nursing puppies receive all the protection they need from their mother's milk. She transfers antibodies from herself through the milk and

you. After the puppy teeth fall out and permanent ones come in, they are all they have to properly chew and digest food. They must be cleaned and scaled regularly.

Plaque and tartar buildup can lead to periodontal disease, which then leads to tooth loss. With regular brushing—twice per week— you can usually avoid costly trips to the canine dentist. Snoopy must learn to allow you access to his mouth and remain very still while scaling. While Snoopy is young you will not see much tartar buildup, but it's a good idea to practice anyway.

Using a child's toothbrush, a finger brush, or even a cloth wrapped around your finger, apply some canine toothpaste and scrub all of Snoopy's teeth from crown to gum. The lower teeth may be more difficult to reach. Be patient and persistent.

Regular medical care is extremely important throughout your puppy's life. Vaccinations and physical exams are part of your dog's lifelong maintenance.

Your well-cared-for puppy will have a long and happy life.

into her pups. However, most puppies begin their weaning process at four weeks, and then need outside protection, first from their breeder and then from your veterinarian.

Puppies are most susceptible to disease-bearing viruses and bacteria during their first few months of life. Their first vaccinations and wormings should be done by their breeder by the time they reach five weeks of age. The next set occurs at seven weeks, just before they are ready to go to their new homes. This will help counteract the stress of leaving their littermates and entering a completely new environment and pack society—your family.

The importance of immediate veterinary care cannot be stressed enough. Before you plan on bringing Snoopy home, arrange an appointment with your veterinarian for a complete physical and his first inoculations. Go directly from the breeder to the vet clinic. If Snoopy has fleas or other parasites, have the vet clinic take care of these *before* you bring him home. All it takes is one flea to cause an infestation.

Many breeders will guarantee their puppies. This does not always mean a refund, but it does mean you have the right to a completely healthy pup. Taking Snoopy to the veterinarian first will ensure that he is 100 percent healthy before you begin to fall in love with him. It would also be a good idea to do this without the children. Children fall in love with puppies faster than lightning hits. Don't bring home an unhealthy puppy unless you have the financial means and time to

properly care for him.

While at the vet clinic Snoopy will be examined from head to tail. Your veterinarian will check his ears, eyes, teeth, heart, take a fecal sample, and give him the first inoculations. He will advise you of anything you must watch out for, such as your puppy's tendency to get ear infections or have eye problems. He will also inform you of the future inoculations and their scheduling. Many veterinarians will also discuss how to control fleas and other parasites. Some will suggest you keep Snoopy away from all other dogs until he receives all of his inoculations. This is wise because, as mentioned earlier, young pups are more susceptible to disease.

Two of the most contagious diseases to puppies other than rabies are parvovirus and coronavirus. These are carried through contact with an infected dog or its feces. Not only are young puppies susceptible, but also older dogs. The symptoms range from diarrhea, vomiting, and lack of energy, to high fever and, if not caught in time, heart failure and death.

Canine distemper is also very contagious and is spread through contact with nasal or eye discharge of an infected dog. This virus can be carried in the air or left on an inanimate object within reach of Snoopy's roving nose. Symptoms include vomiting, diarrhea, and even brain dysfunction, causing your puppy to be aggressive without reason. If not caught in time it also causes death.

The initial inoculations include protection against leptospirosis, a bacterial disease, and parainfluenza, a

respiratory disease. These, like parvovirus, attack the intestinal tract and heart muscles. They spread through contact with contaminated feces and nasal secretions, respectively.

You may be thinking: Wow, that's quite a lot of shots to put poor Snoopy through! Don't fret, most veterinarians use an all-in-one vaccine. Snoopy will receive only one on the first trip to his doctor. When you see the needle, distract your pup by offering him a biscuit or a toy. Stroke him calmly. The needle stings for just a second. Praise Snoopy in a high happy voice throughout the process. This will ensure that he doesn't get vet-clinic phobia.

Two weeks later Snoopy receives the next set of vaccinations and on the following visit he will receive the last ones, which generally includes the rabies vaccine and, if you live in an area where Lyme disease is prevalent, a Lyme vaccine. If you plan on boarding Snoopy at any time, allowing him to play with other dogs, or taking him to obedience classes or shows, he will need a bordetellosis vaccine. This is given as a nasal spray up his nose. Bordetella is also known as kennel cough. An infection causes severe coughing and nasal secretions. It is highly contagious.

Each year you will need to take Snoopy to the veterinarian for a checkup and booster shots to ensure he is protected. The only shot that may not be yearly is the rabies vaccine. After the first year in which Snoopy must receive a booster, the rabies vaccine is administered at three to five year intervals.

TRAIN THAT PUP!

Housetraining is foremost on most new dog owner's agenda. How long will it take and how many carpets will be ruined in the process? Will I have any shoes left? Moreover, will I still be sane?

Housetraining does not just involve making sure your puppy goes potty in the right places. It also means a well-behaved housemate who leaves the chair legs intact and the plants upright—with all the dirt still in the pots.

CRATE TRAINING

The crate is key to ensuring everything in your house remains in good condition, including your relationship with Snoopy. The crate should be a secure, positive place for your puppy. He should walk right into it without any type of force and go there on his own to "get away from it all" if he tires or wishes to avoid commotion.

Proper crate training is the key to making sure it remains Snoopy's bed and not his prison. Begin this training by putting his bed and toys inside the crate. Feeding him in there is also helpful in teaching him that it is a good place. Allow Snoopy free and easy access to the crate. Put the crate where you spend a lot of your time so Snoopy will feel comfortable going inside to rest, knowing you will be there.

The crate will make housetraining easier, because puppies rarely mess where they sleep. If the crate is only large enough for Snoopy to

turn around in, stand, and lie down, you can be assured that he will not mess in it. If it is larger, then he can mess on one side and sleep on the other, making housetraining more difficult.

Some puppies will mess in the crate regardless of size. Usually it is due to someone having put a towel down. Towels soak up urine, so Snoopy won't care about messing on it. Dogs mostly

Crates make housetraining your pet much easier, because dogs do not want to soil where they eat and sleep.

dislike it if the mess is wet against them. So, if the size of the crate is not keeping Snoopy from messing, take out the towel.

Begin using the crate on the first day of Snoopy's arrival. This way you need not come out again. Do not close him in until he is comfortable with the crate. Praise him as he remains inside.

The first time you close Snoopy inside should be short. Remain at the door and open it again within a minute or two.

treat, praise him.

3. If he remains where he picked up the treat, offer another, just a little further inside.

4. If he leaves the crate, put the treat in the same spot again.

Bonding is by far one of the most important building blocks of training. This Golden Retriever youngster revels in the love and attention he gets from his owner.

work on training him to it. He'll simply know that's the way of things. If, however, your pup is wary of the crate, you can throw treats and toys inside. Be patient and remain near the opening. If Snoopy wanders in, praise him and allow him to

You can train Snoopy to go inside on his own by doing the following:

1. Throw a treat near the opening and say, "Kennel" in a soft but demanding tone of voice.

2. As Snoopy goes for the

5. Continue in this manner until your puppy is all the way inside and eagerly awaiting his reward.

6. When Snoopy is comfortable in his crate, close it for a few seconds. Continue to praise him.

7. Open the door and allow him to come out if he wants. Repeat the exercise until he can remain inside for up to five minutes.

8. At this point, leave him alone for a minute, come back and sit near the crate, praising him.

9. Gradually increase his time alone.

Snoopy is now crate trained!

HOUSETRAINING

With crate training accomplished, you can begin housetraining in earnest. The basis of this is scheduling. At first, you'll wonder if you are more trained than the puppy, because you must let Snoopy out at certain times to ensure he does not potty in the house.

Eliminate problems like odors and chewing with products designed specifically for the job. There are sprays that can stop animals from chewing on things that they shouldn't, keeping both your pet and your belongings safe. There are also products that safely eliminate pet odors from clothes, carpets or upholstery and come in non-toxic, biodegradable formulas. Photo courtesy of Francodex Laboratories, Inc.

After a couple months though, he will learn to control himself until his scheduled relief time. The

During housetraining it is important to allow your puppy plenty of time outdoors to attend to his needs.

schedule you use should depend on your own schedule. Most of us have to work; we can't spend the entire day taking a puppy outside. It would be a good idea, however, to try to arrange to take at least a week off, if not two, to acclimate your pup to his new environment. During this time you will be laying down the house rules and learning about each other.

A typical schedule, if you are home, is as follows:

6 a.m.—Take puppy out of crate and go to relief area. Wait until he eliminates.

Feed your puppy. Take Snoopy out again within 15 minutes of his finishing his meal.

Take him out every hour to hour and a half. A smaller breed will need to go out more often than a larger breed.

12 p.m.—Noon feeding— Take him out within 15 minutes of eating. Take Snoopy out every hour to hour and a half.

29

4 p.m.— Evening meal— Take him out within 15 minutes of eating. Take him out every hour to hour and a half. No food after Snoopy's evening meal. No water after 8 p.m.

10-11 p.m.— Last time to relief area.

Regardless of this schedule, your puppy will need to go out after sleeping, playing, or any training sessions. If you can't be with him, put him in his crate. This includes brief trips to the washroom, the front door, or when you are engaged in a television show or neighborly chat. You must either watch him or contain him.

It is important to remember that your puppy wants to please you and with patience will learn what you have to teach him. A Chesapeake Bay Retriever puppy.

PAPER TRAINING

While many of us do not have the luxury of having a spouse at home or the ability to remain home for a week or two, there are other options. However, keep in mind that puppies are like children; left alone for long periods they will get into trouble. If you spend more than eight hours away from home every day, you should rethink getting a puppy. It would not be fair to the dog or yourself.

While not recommended, paper training is another means of making sure Snoopy relieves himself in the appropriate place. Paper training is not recommended because it teaches your puppy that it is okay to go potty in the house. This can lead to many accidents as well as a prolonged housetraining period.

To paper train your puppy do the following:

1. Make a secure enclosure and cover the entire floor in newspaper. A good enclosure can be provided by an exercise pen. These range in height from 24 inches to 48 inches, have six to eight two-foot panels and are easy to store in a closet when not in use.

2. Put Snoopy's bed, water, and toys on one side of the pen.

3. At first your puppy will relieve himself all over the place. Eventually, he will begin to confine his relief area to one side.

4. Begin removing the paper from the areas your pup does not use.

5. If he starts to mess where there isn't paper, cover it again. If not, continue to remove the paper until there are only a few sheets left.

As previously mentioned, puppies will get into mischief if left alone for long periods of time. This includes tearing up the newspaper. Try spraying a bitter-tasting repellent on the edges of the newspaper to avoid this mess. Use just a spritz however, or you may inadvertently repel the puppy from the area.

Another means of ensuring Snoopy recognizes the paper as *the* spot to go is to put it on a metal tray. This not only saves the surface beneath, but also differentiates the surface enough to teach your pup where he can and cannot do his business. Be sure to change the papers as often as you can.

For those of you who plan on first paper training, either because of bad weather or living on the upper floor of a high rise, and then teaching your pup to go outside, think again. Teaching Snoopy it's okay to go in the house, on paper or not, makes the process take far longer. If you wish for your pup to potty outside, teach him to do so immediately, regardless of the

Housebreaking your puppy successfully relies on your patient and consistent reinforcement.

There are basic training commands that every puppy should know how to perform. This Old English Sheepdog puppy is learning the sit-stay command.

weather conditions and how many flights of stairs you'll need to rush down first thing in the morning.

PUPPY KINDERGARTEN

Puppies are not trained the way one trains an older dog. All youngsters need to attend kindergarten. Kindergarten teaches a puppy the meaning of come, sit, down, heel, and stay. Any puppy, from the age of two months, can learn these concepts in a short period of time. While a dog over five months of age will often take up to 20 minutes to learn how to heel, a younger puppy takes only ten. That's because you are dealing with a clean slate—a dog that has not had the time to develop bad habits or willfulness. Also a puppy between the ages of 8 to 12 weeks of age is more eager to learn.

You will need only 10–15 minutes several times per day and plenty of treats. The treats should be soft and easy to break into very small pieces. Freeze-dried liver works well, because a small piece melts in the mouth. You need something like this for several reasons. First of all, you don't want to add lots of calories to Snoopy's diet. Second, if your pup spends time munching, you're taking

his attention away from training. Third, crunchy treats will fill him up quickly, making his attention span shorter.

Puppies have short attention spans. They can work anywhere from 5 to 15 minutes. When their time is up, they simply don't care what type of food you offer—they'd rather go play with their toys or take a nap.

To ensure you get the most out of Snoopy, work in an area where there are few, if any, distractions. He will also work best on an empty stomach and after a long nap. If you have other pets, make sure they're not in the area. Young children can also be too much of a distraction.

THE COME AND SIT COMMAND

Begin Snoopy's training by attaching his leash to his collar. This teaches him that the leash means work time. Then begin by doing the come and sit exercise.

1. Get Snoopy's attention by putting a treat under his nose.

Basic obedience training is necessary for your dog, not only to teach him acceptable behavior, but to keep him safe as well.

Training your puppy will be easier once he is accustomed to wearing a collar and leash.

2. Back up two steps as you say, "Snoopy come."

3. Lure him to you using the food. Bending at the waist or crouching down will be more attractive to him than standing upright.

4. When he arrives directly in front of your feet, praise and give him the food. He should be close enough for you to easily reach down and touch him.

5. Increase the amount of steps backward as you say, "Snoopy, come."

6. When he comes readily, begin having him sit when he arrives.

7. Instead of giving him the food when he arrives, say, "Snoopy, sit" as you lift his nose upward by holding the treat just out of reach of his mouth. Be sure to keep the treat near his nose or he may

jump up trying to reach the food. Lifting his head up has a see-saw effect on his body. His rear end will automatically go down.

8. As soon as he sits, praise and give him the treat.

9. Each person who is to be involved in the pup's training needs to do this exercise.

Round Robin

1. Each trainer should have up to ten pieces of treats. Stand approximately six to eight feet away from each other.

2. One of you should lure Snoopy into a sit in front of you by bending at the waist or crouching as you say, "Snoopy, come." As soon as he sits, praise and offer the treat.

3. Trainer Number 2 then calls out, "Snoopy, come."

4. As soon Snoopy looks at trainer Number 2, he is praised. Your puppy should be praised the entire time he's responding, from the time he looks until he arrives. This encourages him to continue.

5. When Snoopy arrives at trainer Number 2, he is told to sit using the same technique as before. As soon as he sits, Snoopy is praised and given the treat.

6. As soon as Snoopy is given the treat, trainer Number 1 calls him to come.

Most puppies catch on to this game quickly. As Snoopy learns to go back and forth, each trainer should take a step back after every two turns. This increases Snoopy's running space and teaches him to come from a distance.

Round Robin is fun and a great means of ridding your puppy of excess energy. He

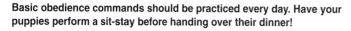

Basic obedience commands should be practiced every day. Have your puppies perform a sit-stay before handing over their dinner!

If you are patient and consistent when training your puppy, you'll have a well-behaved adult dog as a reward. Sammy and his owner practice a come-sit.

learns to come and sit as well as to be attentive. After 15 minutes, he'll take a long nap. Continue working on these exercises a couple of times a day, every day. Make sure you give Snoopy several hours of recovery time between his training sessions. You can do this indoors as well as outside. Once your puppy has a good idea of what to do, you can even add minor distractions such as a toy or two in his path.

THE DOWN COMMAND

After doing the come and sit for four days you can add the down. This should not be done every time your pup comes to you, but after every two or three times. The last thing you'll want is for Snoopy to come to you and lie at your feet. He should always come and sit.

1. After several come and sit exercises, place the treat between the middle finger and thumb of your right hand.

2. Point down with your index finger of the same hand.

3. Lure your puppy down by placing the treat under his nose as you move your hand downward.

4. Say, "Snoopy, down."

5. If Snoopy lowers his head but not his body, apply gentle pressure on his shoulders with your left hand.

6. As soon as his belly touches the ground, praise and give him the treat.

7. The other trainer calls Snoopy to come as soon as he receives his reward.

THE HEEL COMMAND

The down is now added to Snoopy's repertoire of commands. Next is teaching him to walk with you. Up until this time, Snoopy's leash has been dragging behind him. Pick it up and hold it in your right hand. Palm the treats in your left hand. The leash should remain very loose. You will not be pulling on the leash and it may get tangled between Snoopy's feet. Don't worry about the entanglement, Snoopy has been dragging it around enough so that it should not be bothersome.

1. Play Round Robin for a few minutes to get Snoopy into "work" mode.

2. After a nice come and sit, pick up the leash, put it in

The down command is sometimes difficult for puppies to learn because it puts them in a submissive position. This Akita puppy seems to be having no trouble at all!

Successful training relies on your ability to effectively establish yourself as the "leader of the pack" while maintaining a close relationship with your pup. Boxer pup Fanny and her owner practice a heel-sit.

Be sure that you offer your puppy plenty of positive reinforcement and in no time at all he'll be obeying every command. This Dalmatian gets praise for a job well done.

your right hand and turn your body so that Snoopy is along your left side.

3. Put a treat under his nose as you take a step forward with your left leg and say, "Snoopy, heel."

4. As he arrives at your left heel, say, "Snoopy, sit."

5. When he sits, give him praise and the treat.

6. Next time step forward and take two to five steps.

7. Keep luring Snoopy with the food under his nose.

8. When he arrives at your heel, praise him and give him his reward. You should also praise him the entire time he is walking with you. This encourages him to continue.

9. When Snoopy can walk with you up to 20 steps, do a right turn. Keep the food

directly under his nose the entire turn. Stop and tell him to sit as soon as the turn is completed.

10. Keep adding turns, both right and left, as you increase the amount of steps between the stop and sit. Remember to always praise Snoopy as he walks with you. Your praise should be in a high, enthusiastic tone of voice.

Once Snoopy understands the heel and sit, add the down to the heeling exercises. Every three or four stops, ask him to do the down command. It is executed in a similar way to when you did the Round Robin, except for the fact that you are to remain on his right side as you give the command and make sure he follows through.

For Snoopy to remain in heel position—his right shoulder even with your left leg—you need to keep the treat close to your left knee at all times. If Snoopy begins sniffing you need to lure him back to your side by putting the treat under his nose and luring him closer.

As you near the end of a training session, Snoopy may tend to forge ahead of you or stop and play with a leaf. At this time, do a turn, gently tug the leash, and lure him back to your side with the food.

Always end a training session on a positive note. If Snoopy is getting tired he may not listen well, so go back to something that he learned earlier, such as the Round

Robin or come and sit game. Do a couple of rounds then stop.

THE STAY COMMAND

Now comes the time to teach Snoopy to stay. This tends to be the most difficult command to teach a young puppy for they are in constant motion. This is best done through the use of the Round Robin game.

1. Play Round Robin for five minutes. Intersperse the sit and down as usual.

2. Begin the stay exercise by having Snoopy come and sit.

3. When he arrives, hold the treat before his nose and say, "stay."

4. Make him remain only two to three seconds, then give him his reward.

5. Trainer Number 2 then repeats the exercise.

6. Each time you do the stay, add a second or two to the time. This is best calculated by adding, "Good Boys!" On the first stay you use only one "Good Boy!" On the second stay you use two "Good Boys!" and so on.

7. If Snoopy jumps up or tries to grab the treat from you, say, "No!" and make him return to his spot. You may need to step on his leash to prevent him from taking off and going to the next trainer.

8. Work on this exercise until Snoopy can remain seated for up to six or seven "Good Boys!"

This Newfoundland puppy takes a well-deserved break from a hard day of training.

As with all the exercises, intersperse them so that Snoopy does not learn to anticipate what you want. A pattern-trained dog is not an obedience-trained dog.

The next training session you can add the stay command to your heeling exercises. This is slightly more complicated than doing the stay after a come. Timing and consistency are of the utmost importance. There is also a series of three steps you'll have to accomplish before the stay is complete. The first is *time.* Your puppy must be able to remain in one spot up to a minute before step two. Step two is *motion.* Snoopy must learn to remain still as you walk around him. Step three is *distance.* As you move around Snoopy you can gradually increase your distance from him. Since puppies are very insecure you should never move away more than the six to ten feet suggested.

1. Begin your training session by working on heel and sit.

Puppies are naturally mischievous and playful. Basic training will be much more successful if you make it fun and interesting. These Australian Shepherd pups enjoy a day on the beach.

2. After several repetitions make Snoopy sit, place your right hand in front of his face and say, "Snoopy, stay."

3. Step directly in front of him with your right leg first. This is very important because your left leg first means heel. You should be no further than six inches from him, face to face.

4. As you remain in front, praise him and let him sniff the treat in your left hand.

5. Return to heel position, praise Snoopy, and give him the treat. If at any time Snoopy gets up, say, "No" in a low tone of voice and replace him in the exact spot he was originally. Do not allow your puppy to scoot around on his stay or he will never do it properly.

6. Gradually increase the amount of time you remain in front of Snoopy. Remember to use the "Good Boy!" count, but adding "Good Boys" during each stay command. It is important to praise Snoopy throughout his stay. Not only does this reinforce the command in a positive manner, but it also allows you to speak while Snoopy is working.

7. Make sure Snoopy does not get up until you tell him to heel. If he does move after receiving his treat, say, "No" and replace him.

Work on this for up to a week. The stay is difficult for puppies so you must be very patient. When Snoopy can remain in place for a minute do the following:

1. Give the stay command and step in front of your pup.

2. Move a step to each side. Continue to praise Snoopy and give him the treat when you return to heel position.

3. After two to three repetitions, begin to move along both sides of the dog, in a U-shape. With each repetition, move closer to his tail.

4. When Snoopy is content to remain in position with you moving along his sides and in front of him, try going all the way around. Many puppies will get up at this point. They

Very basic training can begin at a relatively early age, once a puppy has been vaccinated and housebroken. However, these young Cocker puppies will have to wait a while until they are ready for the advanced stuff!

The time you invest in training your puppy will benefit the both of you for a lifetime. This pup and his owner practice a come-sit-stay.

have a difficult time turning their heads all the way around so they figure they must scoot around to see you. Always replace Snoopy facing the same direction he was in and go back to moving up and down his sides. Sometimes you'll have to regress to progress.

5. When you can walk one circle around Snoopy with him remaining in place, try two, then three, and so on. Be sure to change directions often. Not only will this teach your pup to accept movement in both directions, but will also prevent you from becoming dizzy.

6. After you can walk around Snoopy at least four times, begin to move out away from him. Do this very gradually, one foot at a time. Within five repetitions you should be

This alert German Shepherd duo eagerly awaits their owner's next command.

able to walk around Snoopy at the end of your leash.

Once Snoopy performs this elongated stay, you can request him to come from his stay position. Be sure to do this from anywhere around him, not just in front. Snoopy needs to understand that he must come from wherever you call him.

Congratulations! You have completed puppy kindergarten.

This pretty Akita puppy demonstrates his good behavior and poses for posterity.

Once your puppy is well trained, there won't be anything you can't do together!

FUN-FILLED DOG DAYS

There are more fun things you and Snoopy can do together than there is time to do them—walking in the woods, camping, fishing, and even horseback riding (of course, Snoopy walks). There are also competitions that specialty or all-breed. The specialty show is limited to one specific breed. In an all-breed show, any breed can enter a class for their breed, provided they are at least six months of age on the day of the show. Neutered animals quality you can enter one of these shows, however, you need to know how to present your pup at his best. If you do not know how, then ask Snoopy's breeder to exhibit your pup for you. Provided Snoopy is of show quality,

There's no telling what life has in store for your puppy; he may be a champion, a therapy dog, a companion—but he'll definitely be your best friend! Staffordshire Bull Terrier puppies.

offer Snoopy a chance to show his stuff. From conformation to obedience to performance, the American Kennel Club sanctions shows all over the country.

CONFORMATION SHOWS

The AKC offers two types of conformation competitions: are not allowed to attend conformation competitions, nor are dogs that have disqualifying faults, such as being oversized. Conformation competition is to showcase a specific breed line's assets. A dog earning a championship is a dog of breedable quality.

If your puppy is of superior your breeder will want to do this anyway, because winning points on the puppies offers their kennel publicity.

After impeccable grooming, a dog is paraded in front of a judge. The judge watches the dogs walk, trot, turn, and stand. He looks at teeth, eye color, bone structure, and

Good conformation should be evident from early puppyhood.

places. An exceptional dog will achieve his points within a short period of time, provided the judge prefers his "type." Judges can be very different on their definitions of the perfect dog. Something as simple as a square versus a narrow head can be disputed among judges, thus making a conformation competition very subjective.

OBEDIENCE TRIALS

There are three levels of obedience trials: novice, open, and utility. In order to obtain a title your dog must qualify with at least 170 points out of a possible 200, under three different judges, at three different shows. Your dog's appearance has nothing to do with the competition, but he must be purebred if compet-

coat. Only the best dogs in the class will place.

To obtain a championship a dog must earn at least 15 points. The amount of points a dog earns in each class depends on how many are in the class and on how he

If your puppy is destined for life in the show ring, part of his basic training must prepare him for handling by judges. This Westie practices striking a perfect pose.

Show ring competition demands that your puppy obey basic commands—this Westie pup and his owner know practice makes perfect!

In a conformation show, dogs are judged on how closely they conform to their breed standard. These English Bulldogs compete for Best of Breed.

ing at an AKC-sanctioned show. However, if you have a mixed breed, the United Kennel Club allows you to compete at their trials. Competitors can also be neutered or spayed. In fact, a neutered dog tends to give a better performance because there are fewer odiferous distractions.

As in conformation classes, Snoopy must be at least six months old. You will find that most of the dogs in this competition are up to a year and a half, for it normally takes at least that long for their dogs to outgrow their puppy pranks.

You begin at the novice level. The title is called Com-

panion Dog, or CD for short. In this class your dog must be able to heel both on and off leash, walk around two people in a figure eight pattern, stand and stay, come off-lead, finish (go around you and place himself into heel position on one command), and remain in a one-minute sit stay and three-minute down stay with dogs on either side of him while you remain 30 feet away.

The next level is open, the Companion Dog Excellent title, or CDX. In this level everything is done off leash. The judge runs you through a heeling pattern that includes at least two stops, right turns and left turns, and several

about turns. Then you must perform an off-lead figure eight around two people, a drop-on-recall, in which you call your dog from 30 feet away, make him lie down when the judge signals you to do so, then finish the recall with your dog coming to sit in front of you.

There are two retrieving exercises in the open class. One plain retrieve, where you tell your dog to stay, throw a dumbbell, send your dog to retrieve it, and have him return to a sit in front of you. This is also done with your dog going over a jump both on the way to retrieve the dumbbell and on the way back to you. Each exercise is topped off with a finish. The next exercise is for your dog to jump over a broad jump without touching it. The jump consists of boards lying only a few inches from the ground. The final exercises are for your dog to remain in a sit stay for three minutes and a down stay for five minutes, lined up with up to 12 other dogs and you out of sight!

The most difficult level is utility. On this level, your dog must perform an entire heeling pattern with only your hand signals to guide him. Then he must remain in a stand stay, while you walk at least 20 feet away, face him and, with hands signals only,

have him lie down, then sit, then come, then finish. As if this wasn't hard enough! He must be able to retrieve a specific object that you point at, retrieve both a metal and leather article that he discerns only by your scent, and leave your side, going to the far side of the ring on command. Once on the other side he must wait for your signal to tell him which of two jumps, either a bar jump or solid jump, to go over on his way back to you. Whew!

If you have both a strong desire to compete and a fantastically motivated dog you can continue on to achieve the UDX, Utility Dog

Excellent and the highest honor of OTCh., Obedience Trial Champion.

PERFORMANCE EVENTS

AKC performance tests include field trials, hunting, herding, lure coursing, and more. Before deciding whether to compete make certain your dog is the appropriate breed. For example, you wouldn't have your sighthound compete with a Labrador Retriever in a hunting test and you wouldn't have a chance with a Golden Retriever in a lure coursing contest with a Rhodesian Ridgeback.

Field trials and hunting trials demonstrate a dog's

Fun and games in the pool or retrieving practice? These two youngsters are having such a good time they can't tell the difference!

This Bloodhound puppy is already putting his scenting abilities to good use.

ability to find game. In the field trial the competitor must work with other dogs doing the same thing at the same time. Separate trials are offered for different breeds such as sporting dogs and hounds. With a "who-can-get-the-duck-first" mentality, there's no hope of a Dachshund competing with a longer-legged Irish Setter. In hunting trials the dogs are judged only against the standard of their own breed, thus it is less competitive.

Herding trials are open to any registered dog in the herding group. These include Border Collies, Australian Shepherds, Corgis, and many more. A competing dog must be at least nine months old. There are two parts to the herding event: Testing for the desire to herd and then testing the ability to herd different types of animals in a variety of settings.

Tracking is very popular with sporting dogs. There are several different levels of competition: TD, or Tracking

Dog title; TDX, or Tracking Dog Excellent title; VST, or Variable Surface Tracking Test; and CT, Champion Tracker. Each level requires more difficult tracks that include crossing over all types of terrain and even crossing over your own track. Dogs must find specific articles with the tracklayer's scent on them. Points are lost for

leaving the track at any time, missing an article, or for taking an extremely long time to finish.

Lure coursing is growing in popularity. Most sighthounds need lots of exercise and lure coursing is just the thing. Breeds such as Whippets, Basenjis, Irish Wolfhounds, Salukis, and Pharaoh Hounds were originally developed for running down fleet prey over long distances. At an AKC lure coursing event, the dogs follow an artificial lure around a course in an open field. All canine competitors must be at least one year old. The titles include JC, Junior Courser; SC, Senior Courser; and FC, Field Champion. Think of how tired your sighthound will be after doing that. Wow, a sound night's sleep!

Some really fun events include agility trials, flyball, and earthdog tests. In agility training your dog gets to go over jumps, climb A-frames, sneak through tunnels, run over a see-saw, and so much more. If your dog loves to play

There's nothing like getting a head start! At only eight weeks old this puppy practices retrieving a training dummy.

ball, flyball is for him. This consists of a specially built machine that your dog jumps on and releases a ball that your dog must catch in the air. In advanced work, the dog must go over jumps both on the way to catch the ball and on his way back to the handler with the ball in his mouth.

In earthdog tests, small terriers and Dachshunds test their small prey hunting ability. They must find two rats that are safely caged in a long narrow tunnel in the ground, usually made of straw bales. They need to show interest by barking and digging for it within three minutes to complete the test.

GAMES

Whether or not you are interested in competing in AKC events there are many things you can teach Snoopy to do around the house and yard that will be fun and, best of all, time consuming for him.

Most puppies enjoy a good game of tug-of-war. While it helps with their teething and offers something you can do with him, this can also be dangerous if done with specific breeds such as German Shepherds, Rottweillers, and many terriers because the dog may demonstrate dominance. You also run the risk of Snoopy thinking your hand is part of the toy—*ouch*! The

best way to know if this game is right for your puppy is to observe his behavior. If he gets *really* feisty when playing, stop. If he growls in a deep tone, stop. If your hand is repeatedly bitten, even accidentally, stop.

Roughhousing is also a popular game. All puppies play rough. They must learn, however, to tone down their roughness when playing with people—especially children. Snoopy should never, *ever* bite, even in play. If he can pounce and jump around without biting then you and he can have a blast. You can initiate the game by getting down on "all fours," sticking your rear end in the air, and

As your puppy grows older, training for any type of competition will allow the two of you to grow closer. Agility trials are fun, growing in popularity, and exciting to watch. The Brittany flies over the bar jump.

bowing down on your elbows. If Snoopy still doesn't get the message, slap your hands against the floor. Without a tail you have nothing to wag, but you're welcome to try anyway. Snoopy will take up a similar stance then leap toward you sideways or bark at you. Gently pull at his legs throwing it just a short distance away. If he goes to get it and brings it back, *fantastic—* you have a natural retriever. If not, don't worry, there are things you can do to increase his retrieving ability.

To make certain Snoopy returns with the toy, tie a light rope to the toy just over and over until Snoopy starts returning to you without your having to retract the toy.

Now that Snoopy fetches, practice throwing different objects such as a ball, bone, Frisbee™, and other fun things. Through this process, Snoopy will tend to fetch his

Thornfield's General Sherman, a seven-month-old Golden Retriever owned by Randy and Eileen Robinson, rummages in his toy box for something safe to play with.

and roll over with him. Be careful that you don't roll on him. Have fun being a puppy.

Another game is to play fetch and find-it. Your pup must be adept at the fetching game before find-it will work. Test Snoopy's fetching ability by first playing with him and his favorite toy and then before you throw it. When your pup puts it in his mouth, draw the toy back to you. Snoopy will have a great time holding onto the moving toy and easily return to you. When he does, praise him and play with him and the toy. When he drops the toy, throw it again. Repeat this game favorite toy the fastest. Now you know which toy he'll do anything for. Most retrievers opt for a tennis ball or plush toy, while many working breeds prefer bones and things they can dig their teeth into. The reason is that retrievers were bred to "soft-mouth" game, while working

These two littermates grapple for top dog. It will be up to you to teach your puppy appropriate ways to play with his human family.

dogs were bred for protective duties.

The find-it game begins by making Snoopy remain in place while you put the toy a short distance away from him. Have someone in your family hold him and allow him to see where you put it. When you return to Snoopy, tell him to "Find-it!" He'll go retrieve his toy and bring it back to you. Praise him enthusiastically.

Repeat this a few times and then partially hide the toy behind a table or chair. Snoopy should still be able to see it, but not all of it. When he can retrieve his toy reliably, go for the next step. Hide the toy behind something.

If you don't keep your puppy busy with fun and games, he'll find mischief. This pup nips at his mom's ear to see if he can interest her in some playtime!

This trio of Akita pups enjoys a game of tag in the snow.

them for you? Once your pup learns how to play the find-it game, you can begin teaching him to find specific items. This is done by naming objects as he plays and retrieves them. Not only will this be handy for finding things you lose, but if you plan on training Snoopy to help the physically challenged, he's well on his way to becoming a good service dog.

A healthy and well-mannered puppy is a joy to own. Snoopy will need to be cared for from his nose to his tail and everything in between. He needs proper nutrition, grooming and training for a full and happy life. Snoopy should be part of your family. And, as every youngster needs to learn the rules, a dog, loyal and forever loving, wants nothing less.

Up to this point Snoopy has been able to watch as you hide his toy. He knows immediately where to look for it. Now, have someone occupy him in a game or take him into another room. Hide the toy, return to Snoopy and tell him to find it. The first thing he'll do is investigate where he retrieved it earlier. Not finding it (provided you didn't put it there), he'll begin sniffing around. Snoopy has begun tracking down his toy. Depending on how good his nose is, he'll eventually find it and return it to you for another game.

As Snoopy progresses you can hide the toy in more difficult places such as under a bush outside or behind the bed. The more difficult you make the game, the more Snoopy will want to play. Best of all, he remains stimulated and occupied at the same time!

Ready to try those tracking tests? If you intend to eventually try them, this is the best way to start your pup in the right direction.

Planning on attending obedience trials? Both the retrieve and find-it game are exercises used in several levels of obedience trials.

Lose your keys? What's better than for Snoopy to find

The attachment that forms between children and puppies is legendary. Train your puppy well, so he can be a good companion for a lifetime. Ryan Kleeman and his Greater Swiss Mountain puppy are the best of friends.

LOOKING AHEAD

For the next six to ten months you and Snoopy will be learning about each other and adjusting to new situations. Each month Snoopy will be going through different developmental stages each bringing new challenges. Teething and hormonal changes will both play major roles in his behavior patterns.

between weeks seven and ten. He will be more accepting and will easily bond with his new family pack. At this age Snoopy will also be very dependent on his new family. He'll want to always be by your side. Thus you may be tempted to not keep him on a leash in a quiet open area. However, it is always a good

that he is afraid of.

Let's use the example of Snoopy being afraid of getting into the car. He remembers the car took him away from his siblings and into the nightmare of sharp objects and strange people. The best means of overcoming the fear is to coerce him to sniff and explore. Placing treats in a

Although some traits are inherited within a breed, every puppy is an individual. These Mastiff friends agree!

There are three distinct periods in puppy development. The first is the social development period that occurs between the ages of 6 to 12 weeks. At this time, Snoopy is learning about new people and environments. The prime time to move him from his litter to a new home is

idea to get him used to the idea of wearing one, even if you don't need to use it.

The second stage is the fear imprint period. It can occur both at four months and again at nine months. At this time everything can be scary. Make certain Snoopy is never forced to confront something

line toward the object can be helpful. Taking the time to sit near the car door while Snoopy rests nearby is also helpful. He has learned to trust you. If he sees you are unafraid, he will get the message.

The third stage of development is adolescence. What

A properly socialized puppy will be able to get along with all the members of a household. This French Bulldog and his friend like to cuddle!

about himself, testing his boundaries.

Canine behavioral studies have shown that dogs may age 18–21 years (behaviorally) in their first year of life, and five years for every year beyond that. Thus, their first year entails many changes.

The most obvious change is in their sexual activity. By the time Snoopy reaches five months of age, his hormones are flowing and he will react to enticing scents. This reaction can change his normal easygoing behavior into anything from restlessness to aggression. The younger he is, the more you might see just restlessness and playfulness. If he's about seven months or more he will become more on edge and the possibility of aggression increases. Female dogs do not go through such intense personality changes. While they can experience estrus anytime from 6 to13 months of age, they do not

once was a well-behaved puppy eager to please you will turn into a rambunctious, assertive dog who ignores your commands. Snoopy will begin noticing things he had previously ignored, such as other dogs.

Canine adolescence normally begins around five months and can last anywhere from the age of ten months to a year and a half. Not only is this a puppy's peak energy period, but Snoopy will feel very confident

Your puppy's relationship with his littermates is an essential one. He will learn to interact with other dogs by playing with his siblings.

With the proper training and attention, your puppy can become all that you want him to be—the perfect pet and a valued family member.

During adolescence your previously adorable puppy may appear lanky and gawky. Have no fear, all puppies pass through this stage and will soon be lovely adults!

necessarily become aggressive. However, they may become restless, nervous, and flakier than usual, and for example, may not readily listen to commands. They also tend to urinate more often, especially if in estrus, sort of as a means of letting the neighborhood dogs know the time is right.

As you most likely obtained Snoopy to be a family pet, you should have him sexually altered before he exhibits these disruptive behaviors. Whether male or female, Snoopy can be neutered or spayed at six to seven months of age. This operation is not traumatic. In most cases, you can pick your pup up the evening of or the morning after the operation. Be responsible and neuter your pet! Snoopy will be a better, more attentive family member.

Besides neutering there are other things you can do to make sure Snoopy remains in your good graces and learns the house rules. Exercise is the most important thing you can offer him while his energy level is soaring. If you work during the day, take Snoopy on a brisk walk just before leaving. Do another when you return home. If you remain home during the day you should take the time to exercise your pup. Go to a park or ball field. Let him run. If you know of any friendly dogs in the neighborhood, get in touch with their owners and arrange a time to meet. Snoopy will love nothing better than to play with another dog. This is the best means of wearing down his energy without having to wear yourself out. After a long run Snoopy will listen better. Plus, there are great benefits! You can catch up on the neighborhood gossip.

Another thing you should do is to remain consistent and maintain your leadership position. Snoopy will be testing your authority. Do not allow him to misbehave. Also, any time you feed him or offer treats, make him earn them. This is easily done by having him sit or lie down before he gets his meals.

The last thing you should do is give Snoopy something if he barks at you. The bark is a demand for attention. You should only give him attention when you choose to do so.

All puppies need to chew. Provide your puppy with safe and healthy Nylabone® toys for hours of fun and enjoyment.

Your puppy will look to you, his owner, to take care of all his needs. This Cavalier King Charles Spaniel takes time to smell the flowers.

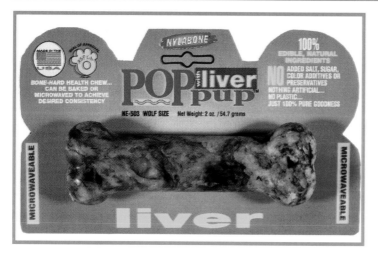

POPpups™ are healthy treats for your puppy. When bone-hard they help to control plaque build-up; when microwaved they become a rich cracker which your puppy will love. The POPpup™ is available in liver and other flavors and is fortified with calcium.

The bark should be corrected by placing your hand around his muzzle, looking him in the eyes and saying, "No!" in a low tone of voice. Continue looking in his eyes until he looks away first. Never, ever look away first. Snoopy will interpret this as submission.

Teething will drive Snoopy bonkers. At three months of age his front teeth will be falling out while his adult teeth take over. He'll want to rip things up and gnaw on wood. Snoopy may even try mouthing your hands. None of these behaviors should be allowed or you are starting off on the wrong paw. Watch Snoopy at all times and take away anything he's not supposed to have, replacing it with one of his toys. His little teeth are sharp but the bigger teeth will cause even more damage due to increased jaw pressure. Regardless of age, chewing on the wrong thing is not cute. Always have at least three toys wherever Snoopy is

spending his time. Whether you are with him in the kitchen, family room, or he is in his crate, he needs to keep his mouth busy. Rotating his toys is also a great means of keeping him interested in them. Offer three one day and a different three the next day.

When Snoopy reaches five months, his back teeth will fall out, replaced with his adult molars. Not only will the puppy teeth be replaced, but new teeth are coming into his jaw, way in the back and they are loose. This causes no end of discomfort. Snoopy will want to chew on hard objects such as table legs and corners of walls. Once again, you must watch him closely and replace the bad "chew toy" with one of his own. You should also find positive things to help him alleviate his pain. Ice cubes work nicely, as does a frozen washcloth. Give these things freely. It will save more stress than you can imagine. If Snoopy is picky

about the ice cube, try using chicken bouillon in the ice cube tray and make puppy pops. Not a single pup will refuse this treat.

Teething is the reason behind much of Snoopy's destructive behavior. However, there may be other reasons he is misbehaving, such as separation anxiety. A puppy used to having someone home with him for a long period of time that is suddenly gone most of the day will suffer severe anxiety. This can be avoided by gradually increasing his time alone and providing him with attractive toys. Make your leaving a

A healthy and tasty treat for your puppy because they love cheese is CHOOZ™. CHOOZ™ are bone-hard but can be microwaved to expand into a huge, crispy dog biscuit. They are almost fat free and about 70% protein.

The moment a puppy walks into your life, it will never be the same. The adventures you'll have and the bond you'll share will last a lifetime.

The Hercules™ is made of very tough polyurethane. It is designed for puppies who are extremely strong chewers. The raised dental tips massage the gums and mechanically remove the plaque they encounter during chewing.

pleasant experience by giving him something special such as a Nylafloss™ or a Galileo™ Bone by Nylabone®. When you come home don't overdo your greeting. The last thing Snoopy needs is a tearful goodbye or hello. This increases his anxiety.

If Snoopy spends a lot of time outside you may notice a few other annoying canine behaviors such as digging, chewing plants, and barking excessively. Digging is a favorite doggy pastime. If Snoopy is left outside without anyone to play with, no books to read, and no blocks to build space ships, digging is all that's left, especially if it's really hot. A freshly dug hole is far cooler to lie in than the hot earth above ground. A hole dug under a

plant is even better becuase the plant helps offer shade.

The best means of overcoming the problem is to not

leave Snoopy outside for long periods of time. When he does go outside, go with him. If he begins to dig or chew on a plant you can easily correct him by pulling him away from the spot and saying, "No!" in a low tone of voice. Throw a ball for him to get his mind off of digging and onto another activity.

While adolescence will be trying and frustrating, do not give up. In a few more months Snoopy will be a great pet and you will be able to trust him in the house. Remember, Snoopy will live to be anywhere from 11 to 17 years of age. Every child needs to learn about his environment in order to grow into a responsible adult. Snoopy, as an eternal child, will always be looking for his parents weaknesses. Remain consistent *throughout* his life and he'll be a great pet. What's a few months of having to be watchful? You're forming a relationship unlike any other and it's worth it!

The Galileo™ is the toughest nylon bone ever made. It is flavored to appeal to your puppy and has a relatively soft outer layer. It is a necessary chew toy and doggy pacifier.

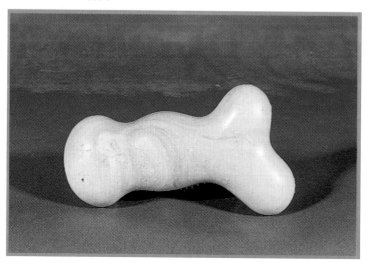

Although your new puppy won't need a highchair, he will need plenty of time and attention from you—just like a baby!

A basket full of love and surprises await every new puppy owner. Enjoy!

SUGGESTED READING

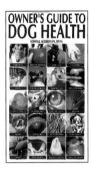

TS-249
Owner's Guide to Dog Health
Dr. Lowell Ackerman, DVM
224 pages, over 190 color photos

TS-214
Skin and Coat Care for Your Dog
Dr. Lowell Ackerman, DVM
432 pages, over 300 full-color photos

TS-252
Dog Behavior and Training
Edited by Dr. Lowell Ackerman, DVM
292 pages, over 200 full-color photos

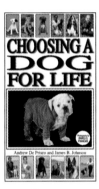

TS-257
Choosing a Dog for Life
Andrew DePrisco and James Johnson
384 pages, over 700 full-color photos

TS-258
**Training Your Dog for Sports
and Other Activities**
Charlotte Schwartz
160 pages, over 100 color photos

TS-293
Adopting a Great Dog
Nona Kilgore-Bauer
128 pages, over 100 color photos